WHERE ARE WE GOING?

WHERE ARE WE GOING?

UNNATURAL BEHAVIOR

Michael Walker

 iUniverse

WHERE ARE WE GOING?
UNNATURAL BEHAVIOR

iUniverse books may be ordered through booksellers or by contacting:

iUniverse
1663 Liberty Drive
Bloomington, IN 47403
www.iuniverse.com
1-800-Authors (1-800-288-4677)

ISBN: 978-1-4917-8802-8 (sc)
ISBN: 978-1-4917-8803-5 (e)

Library of Congress Control Number: 2016901587

Print information available on the last page.

iUniverse rev. date: 02/23/2016

The year is 2083, and in the House of Representatives it's standing room only, as lawmakers find themselves challenged to address the problem of acts committed by serial killers and others. They are going back and forth in indecision, while attempting to address the epidemic that is killing thousands of women, men, and children, by those having "sexual feelings or activities that involve dead bodies" or obsession with and usually erotic interest in or stimulation by corpses", necrophilia according to Webster.

The bill, up for vote, referred to as, we'll call it Proposal 25a. This is the focus of the debate.

It addresses the legalization of necrophilia, to stop the desecration of corpses. Those who practice this type of behavior are referred to as necrophiliac's.

Proposal 25a was passed by the Senate with a majority vote a few weeks earlier. Some of those in favor of the new law want to legalize necrophilia believing that this would put an end to the slaughter of innocent men, women and children.

Hundreds of necrophilia demonstrators and their supporters, armed with picket signs and waving the American flag, are positioned just outside of the White House and Capitol Hill. They are accompanied by their spokesperson who we will call, Mr. Ridgeway III, a third generation decedent of one of the most notorious necrophilia serial killers in history, Gary Ridgeway, known as The Green River Killer. Determined and serious about their fight, we hear them in the media saying things like "We are not hurting anyone, we just want our rights". These demonstrators are speaking to people like CNN Anchor Anderson Cooper III, Fox News Political correspondent Bill O'Reilly III, and MSNBC news correspondent, Ed Shultz III, and others.

The increase in necrophilia activity has thrust this debate to the forefront of the media even though the discussion has been going on for some five years now.

What has caused the spike in necrophilia crimes? Well roughly about thirty years ago, Proposal 18b was passed making zoophilia legal. Proposal 18b legalizes crimes of zoophilia, the erotic addiction and passion for animals which often lead to a person's arousal or sexual excitement with real or even imagined contact with animals. Zoophiliacs often have sex or sexual relationships with animals. Zoophiliacs thirty years ago also demonstrated and conducted protests on Capital- Hill seeking their right to have sexual relationships or even to marry animals.

A week prior to this day, after going back and forth in the House of Representative, just like similar bills that proceeded it, Proposal 25a passed through the House unanimously as it also passed thru the senate a few weeks earlier.

Now there is only one thing left. The President of the United States must sign off on it, which he or she agreed to do if the law passes thru the House of Representatives. Soon after the House of Representative passed Proposal 25a, the President immediately has signed off as well. It is done!!! Necrophilia is now legal. This is a victory for these sick and twisted people and others who support it.

The President's rational for this was one that sounds all too familiar, with comments like, Well, I don't do it, and my kids, friends, or family members don't do it. These people are not hurting anyone and if passing this bill would save lives, than we need to pass this. Besides, it's the right thing to do as the number of those practicing this type of behavior is reaching the millions.

The thing to keep in mind here is that numbers control politics, politics control politicians,

politicians control laws, and laws control people. That being said allows you to look at things from a politician's point of view. In order to get re-elected, you have to please the people and the majority rules. And the majority wants this law passed, so what do you do as a politician? Do you stand up for your beliefs, or do you conform? Yes you guessed it; most will conform because if they didn't, they wouldn't have long political careers.

Strange huh? Sick Huh? Unbelievable Huh? Twisted Huh? I bet those of you who are reading this will also say unlikely, huh? We will never go this far, huh?

What if I told you that your grand-parents and possibly your parents over 30 years ago never thought we would see same sex marriage legalized. What if I also told you that when the idea of same sex marriages came up, your grand-parents and possibly your parents used the same phrases to describe same sex marriages, phrases like strange, twisted, sick and unlikely. But here we are, over 30 plus years later and more and more states are legalizing same sex marriages and it's only a matter of time before all 52 states legalize it.

So where are we going with this or better yet, where am I going with this? How far is too far? When will we, or it stop, how liberal are we going to become in future years. I'll answer that in a later segment of the book, but let's look at how this whole thing started.

INTERRACIAL MARRIAGE

In 1967, interracial marriages finally became legal in all states except for one, Alabama after a long, drawn-out fight in the capital. So how did they get there?

It started long before the civil rights movement and even slavery. But before I get into details on this, let's look at the perception of those who lived before it became legal and what they were thinking back then.

After the civil war, the general consensus was that everybody must stick with their own kind and that mixing races was unacceptable and unnatural behavior. Those who participated in interracial relationships were mostly doing it in secrecy. The majority of those living in that time frowned upon those who would participate in such activities. Whites in this country, who thought they were the dominant species and who did deemed people of color to not be human beings, used some of the same phrases that I used earlier to describe necrophilia, to describe interracial marriages, like strange, twisted, sick, and unlikely. Consider Section VI of the Louisiana Black Code of 1724: which forbid white subjects, of both sexes, to marry with the blacks, under the penalty of being fined and subjected to some other arbitrary punishment. Marriage between whites and blacks was not only forbidden, but also punishable. Even priests and those who sanctioned such a marriage would be dealt with punishment. These 54 codes or articles were developed to regulate interactions or relations between colonists and slaves. Also called, the slave codes, or Louisiana Code noir, or slave code remained effective until 1803 when the United States gained possession of Louisiana.

Those who would dare get caught participating in such interracial marriage were subjected to paying fines, assaults, imprisonment and in some cases death. Even if you didn't have a problem with others dating outside of the race, and it was not something you would do, you would have certainly not voiced your opinion, and definitely not taken a stand.

You see, to those that lived before and especially after the civil war (whites and blacks) particularly in the south, this would be something that would never become legal. Not in this country. Interracial marriage would never be allowed. No law would be passed approving such behavior.

Miscegenation is a term that refers to mixing of races. It was invented in 1863. However anti-miscegenation laws that prohibited marriage or even sexual intercourse between a black and a white person were created well before then.

After the Civil War, slaves were freed. People were starting to date or at least attempt to date and have open relationships and sexual relationships with those outside their race. Today we see interracial couples in most areas and we don't even give it a second look, it's the new normal. So here we are in 2015 and interracial marriage is legal, alive, and working without resistance. It's very common and acceptable.

Now by no means am I saying that this is wrong, sick and twisted because we are all live human beings. We are of opposite sexes, as the source intended it to be; we are just of different pigmentations. I'm simply using it as a starting point to illustrate how we don't accept something early on, then our thoughts and convictions change. We then grow to accept 'unacceptable' things over time. So following are some details.

In 1664, Maryland passed a law banning white women from marrying black men. This was well before the USA became a nation and well before the Revolutionary War. Then in 1691, "The Commonwealth of Virginia bans all interracial marriages", this was the actual start of this perception. We then fast forward to 1780, where the first steps to abolish slavery was set in place by the state of Pennsylvania who repeals the law passed in 1691. It failed. Things pretty much remained the same for more than 50 years. So before we move forward, let's review how people saw mixing races back then.

It was very uncommon for whites and blacks in this country to marry or even try to get married outside of their race. Blacks were mainly slaves, and even whites who were in control, did not have the right to marry their slaves or any blacks for that matter.

If we really examine how things really were back then, we might even say that the numbers of those who were interested in marrying outside the race were few and far between. The number of those interested in such behavior was very low. I can't tell you how low those numbers were, but if you can imagine the perception of those for instance that are interested in say zoophilia (having sexual relations or relationships with animals) right now in 2015, then I would think those numbers are similar.

You can see here, the correlation between what is common now verses what was deemed unacceptable, unlikely, sick, twisted, and strange. You see how those living in the distant past (relatively speaking) frowned heavily on interracial marriages. In fact, I bet if you were to sit down with the average white person, not even from the south back then, they would have used these same phrases, and probably have thrown you out of their house. I even believe that if you would have spoken to slaves back then, they might have had the same perception, and maybe even thrown you out of their slave quarters. You see it was uncommon and unnatural behavior to engage in interracial marriage and in interracial intercourse back then. There were only small pockets of people who would openly risk their lives by participating in such activities.

I understand that marriage is a union between a male and female of the human race. I believe that had I been alive then and had to live by the standards of the 1700's, I too, would not have condoned such behavior. I too, like everyone else back then, probably would have deemed it unnatural due to the perception that it was something our ancestors were against, and because it was not commonplace back then.

So we fast forward to 1843. Interracial marriage has become a little bit more common. The fight to repeal previous laws banning interracial marriages takes off. That year, in 1843, Massachusetts makes a second stand to repeal the law, but it fails.

Then in 1883, after the Civil War, the case of Pace vs. Alabama goes to the Supreme Court and it rules unanimously that state law bans Tony Pace and Mary Cox, an interracial couple from marrying. They were both arrested under section 4189, each sentenced to seven years.

Then in 1912, Rep. Seaborn Roddenberg, a Georgia Democrat, makes a second attempt to revise the constitution to ban interracial marriages in all 50 states.

Following that in 1922, "Congress passes the Cable Act", this is a law which stripped away the citizenship of any United States citizen who married someone referred to as "an alien ineligible for citizenship". Asian-Americans were the target at this time because Supreme Court's ruled in the case, United States vs. Thind, that Asian Americans are not white and therefore cannot legally become citizens because they are not white. The U.S. citizen that married an alien ineligible for citizenship lost their citizenship. Now although when we speak about interracial marriages, we often think about black and white couples, but there were also others in this country back then that frowned upon other race mixing as well. So as we see from the 1922 law, interracial marriage was un-natural behavior for other ethnic backgrounds as well.

We move on to 1928, where Senator Coleman Blease, a democrat and former governor of South Carolina, who was also a proud member of the Klu Klux Klan, made another unsuccessful attempt to revise the constitution to ban interracial marriages.

Let's take a look at where we were at that point. Interracial marriages in the 1920's were becoming more and more common. Although there were some who had no problem with it even in the 1800's, interracial marriage was starting to become widely accepted. More and more people were coming out in support of it, mainly because more and more people were doing it, or knew someone who was.

You see, it went from widely unacceptable, to commonplace over a period of time. What most had deemed as unnatural behavior was becoming more natural. If you were to ask people living in the 1600's to late 1800's, they would have never expected it to go that far, meaning getting to the point where hundreds of thousands of people were marrying out of their own race to the point where we have to take the fight to the Capital.

From the 1600's to the mid 1800's, there were only small pockets of people who participated in that type of activity and there was not a strong need to object to it because those people were considered sick and twisted and nobody wanted to be around them. So they arrested them, persecuted them and even caused physical harm to them. Can you see where I'm going with this?

Fast forward to the 1967 movie, *Guess Who's Coming to Dinner,* that was produced and directed by Stanley Kramer, and written by William Rose. This movie featured great actors, Sidney Poitier and Katharine Hepburn. At this point we are geared toward a showdown to allow interracial marriages to become legal in every state; it has hit mainstream media in film.

Guess Who's Coming to Dinner depicts an African American family doctor who falls for and gets engaged to one of his patient's daughter (a white female). Both of their parent's dads strongly oppose the marriage based on values instilled in them from their previous generation. Eventually both fathers decide to let down guards and support the marriage - primarily because the times call for them to do so.

Here is the thing about change that some reading this book will not see. Time determines what becomes acceptable based on the number of people doing a particular thing. Then when everyone, or the majority of people start doing 'that thing' even if it is against our morals, or the way we were taught, then we just accept it.

Another thing to remember is the infamous kiss between Captain Kirk and Uhora on Star

Trek. It was around the same time frame as Guess Who's Coming to Dinner. This kiss stirred up even more controversy because that was actually on TV, and not in a movie. This caused outrage among most whites in this country. People knew this was going on in society but to actually see it on a TV show made them aware that they must now deal with the very thing they wanted to put out of mind. TV programming had such a powerful influence over popular culture at the time.

You see, once a particular behavior is brought to the big screen or even television, children and adults see the programs which impact the manner in which we view the actions seen. We begin to mellow down and accept something as natural behavior that we previously would not have accepted as natural.

In the case of Loving vs Virginia in 1967, ironically the same year the movie came out, the Supreme Court ruled in favor of Loving overturning Pace vs Alabama, stating the state law violates the Fourteenth Amendment to the US Constitution.

Chief Justice Earl Warren wrote:

"There is patently no legitimate overriding purpose independent of invidious racial discrimination which justifies this classification. The fact that Virginia prohibits only interracial marriages involving white persons demonstrates that the racial classifications must stand on their own justification, as measures designed to maintain White Supremacy..."

"The freedom to marry has long been recognized as one of the vital personal rights essential to the orderly pursuit of happiness by free men ... To deny this fundamental freedom on so unsupportable a basis as the racial classifications embodied in these statutes, classifications so directly subversive of the principle of equality at the heart of the Fourteenth Amendment, is surely to deprive all the State's citizens of liberty without due process of law. The Fourteenth Amendment requires that the freedom of choice to marry not be restricted by invidious racial discrimination's. Under our Constitution, the freedom to marry, or not marry, a person of another race resides with the individual and cannot be infringed by the State."

Now this is where interracial marriages became legal in every state, except Alabama. They didn't make interracial marriages legal in until the year 2000. Although, they stop enforcing the law decades ago, they continued to stop similar measures to repeal it, even up to 1999.

Now one thing here is important to note, is that even one of those who oppose the law said he would vote on it, State Rep. Phil Crigler at the time stated "although he personally opposes interracial marriages, he will vote for the bill. He said the bill was just racial grandstanding, since the law prohibiting such marriages is not enforced".

"The virtue of this (bill) passing or failing it not going to change things in Alabama at all." Now let's consider that for a second. Remember what I said earlier, numbers control politics, politics control politicians, politicians control laws, and laws control people. This is a clear-cut example of conforming to the people, even if you don't believe or support the bill.

So now where are we? We are now in a comfortable place where interracial marriages are common. We see interracial couples everywhere we go and most of us don't even think twice about it. If it were 70 plus years ago, all parties involved would definitely have turned heads and possibly been arrested, assaulted and in some cases murdered. I have even dated outside the race and could not imagine not having the right to do so. But if my great, great grandparents were still alive, the family possibly might have dis-owned me or cut me out. I am sure they would have shared their concerns with me stating that interracial relationships would be unacceptable, twisted, or even un-natural behavior to them. It would probably even be the same for you no matter what background you come from. Yes, there are still those who frown on interracial marriage, but their numbers are now decreasing. They are few and far between, unlike back in the day when they were the majority.

In the late 1960's, it was really starting to hit the fan. The hippie movement preached free love and there was a lot of interracial mixing taking place. I'm sure they were even in the media saying things like "We are not hurting anyone, we just want our rights."

What was unnatural and unacceptable, is now natural, and acceptable.

According to the Pew Research Center, in a June 4, 2010 report entitled, *One-in-Seven New U.S. Marriages is Interracial or Interethnic*

"Rates of intermarriages among newlyweds in the U.S. more than doubled between 1980 (6.7%) and 2008 (14.6%)... Rates more than doubled among whites and nearly tripled among blacks...for both Hispanics and Asians, rates were nearly identical in 2008 and 1980."

"Most Americans say they approve of racial or ethnic intermarriage..."2% not just in the abstract, but in their own families. More than sixty percent say that interracial marriage "would be fine" if a member of their family said they were going to get married to someone from any of the three major ethnic/race groups other than their group.

More than 35% (a third of adults) reveal having a family member that is married to a person of a different race.

We now accept something as commonplace that we never envisioned accepting as commonplace 60 plus years ago. And it's as normal as a regular marriage.

So what's next? Where are we going? Who's on deck or stepping up to the plate? Well, how about we look at where we are now. Follow me! Have you been reading the papers and watching the news? I have, and I see a trend. I see something coming into play that I could not ever have dreamed of as a youth, but here we are. Are you following me yet? Where are we now?

SAME SEX MARRIAGES

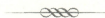

Now this is where things begin to get a little tricky. Allow me to start by saying that I am not bashing gays or lesbians. In fact, I know plenty of gays and lesbians, and have worked with many of them in past years. By nature, they are some of the nicest, coolest, and kindest people you ever want to meet. So again, let me state that this is not an attack or basing session.

Now, on the flip side, I realize that if you are a Bible believer, then you would say that being of the same sex and marrying is un-natural behavior. Let me also state that if you are a Bible believer and reading this, then you know not to judge anyone as God is the judge of us all. You also know that the Bible can be interpreted differently from person to person, so scripture may not completely support your position. You can only pray for and love those who you believe to be living an ungodly lifestyle. It is not our place to judge.

Let me re-iterate. I am not speaking badly of gays or lesbians. I am also not comparing them to what is to come in later chapters. I am simply making a symbolic point. So please don't get offended if you are gay or lesbian. This is just a correlation from something that was not unacceptable, to what could become acceptable at a later date. By no means are you in any future category on what is to come. Neither are those who are referred to in interracial marriage section included in the category of what is to come, for that matter. I do have grounds for writing this book and I'm sorry to say, that your fight will be a pivotal fight for what could eventually happen in this country and throughout the rest of the world. I can't judge any of you. I have my own problems and I have to get myself right with my maker. So don't let my opinion or writing cause a rift between me and you and your fight. In saying that, let me continue.

So let me begin by saying, that about 30+ years ago, if I had told you or anyone living back then, that same sex marriages would be legal in some states, you would have probably called me crazy. Perhaps you would have used some of the same terms like, not possible, unacceptable, unbelievable, strange, and twisted. Yet look around. Here we are on the verge of getting same sex marriages legal in every state. Give it a few years. This is where we are now. So how did it start? Well let's take a look.

Gays and Lesbians have been fighting for their rights for hundreds of years now, just like those who had the fight the interracial marriage battle. They were in the closest and were few in numbers, at least as far as we knew. The fight for same-sex marriage really started to gain momentum as states progressed into legalizing interracial marriages. Once interracial marriages came into full circle, then the next fight began.

In the late 1960's, more and more gays and lesbians were coming out protesting and demanding to have the same rights as heterosexual couples. Prior to the late 1960's, they were scrutinized, ridiculed, assaulted, imprisoned, and in some countries put to death for this behavior, because just like interracial marriages, this was considered unnatural behavior. Most were ashamed to even let people know they were gay or lesbian. It wasn't deemed unnatural behavior to just christian's, but even to other sects, colonies, races, and religions, including Muslims.

The Stonewall riots in 1969 was a major event in the beginning here in the United States. This was a pure gay rights movement that unified gays and lesbians and prompted the next fight following the interracial marriage issue. Around the same time decriminalizing homosexual behavior began in England, Canada and a few other countries. In the early 1970's, gays and lesbians came out of the closest like never before.

They even began to enter politics. In 1977, Harvey Milk became the first openly gay man to be elected to public office. He won a seat on the San Francisco Board of Supervisors. Eleven months later, he was assassinated. So just like most fights in this country, the gay and lesbian movement had a martyr. Someone who gets assassinated which furthers the fight. And in this fight, I'm sure there were more and possibly more to come.

The protest began to become more and more intense and the number of those practicing in such behavior grew rapidly. By the end of the 1980's, those who were gay or lesbian were not ashamed to be seen. To have family members, friends and even the world know that there were gay or lesbian was no longer a shameful experience. I am sure that the gay and lesbian community were making comments in the media like, we are not hurting anyone. We just want our rights.

You see, if you look at the plight of this so far, just as the interracial couples were ashamed and embarrassed to let people know what they were up too, the exact same thing took place with gays and lesbians.

Now fast forward to the early 1990's, the case of Baehr verse Lewin. In 1993, "the judge ruled that states have to give a concrete and compelling reason why gays should not have the same legal right to marry as heterosexual couples".

The case of Baehr verse Lewin actually influenced The Defense of Marriage Act a few years later. This was a law designed to counter same sex marriages and stop or slow down the fight. This was also a law that gave those who deemed same sex marriages as un-natural behavior a strong stand. This act actually stalled the fight for same sex marriages but it came up a few years later in the late 1990's.

The Defense of Marriage Act states that "for the purpose of Federal Law, marriage was only possible for one man and one woman". This federal law gave individual states the right to refuse to recognize same-sex marriages that was granted under the laws of other states. '"No State... shall be required to give effect to any public act...or judicial proceeding of any other State...respecting a relationship between persons of the same sex that is treated as a marriage under the laws of such other State...".

In 1999, Civil Unions were formed. The purpose of these Civil Unions was to give same sex couples the same equal rights as heterosexual couples.

Fast forward to 2003, a Massachusetts Supreme court judge ruled "that gays had the same rights to marriage as heterosexual couples". Then in May of 2004, Massachusetts became the 1st state in the Union to approve same sex marriages. Connecticut soon followed and in

2008, California got on board. This made a huge impact.

The other determining factor to look at is mainstream media. Yes, mainstream media. If you recall in the previous chapter, we referred to about a movie "Guess Who's Coming to Dinner" and a scene from a TV series, "Star Trek". Those two media events, without a doubt, helped the fight to legalize interracial marriages in the late 1960's. So what impact is media now having in regard to same sex marriage? Well, let's take a look.

To the best of my knowledge, or at least as far as I can remember, gays and lesbians have been referenced in film quite often over the past 20+ years. The 1st reference of film that comes to my mind was *The Crying Game* back

33

in 1992, starring Stephen Rea, Jaye Davison, Miranda Richardson and Forest Whitaker. This was the first time I ever remember hearing about this this type of lifestyle on the big screen. I'm sure there were others back then, but I wasn't looking for them. Due to my heterosexual lifestyle and Christian beliefs, of course, I had no interest.

Another blockbuster smash that showed the same sex marriage theme was, *Brokeback Mountain*, Released in 2006, this movie starred Heath Ledger, Jack Gyllenhaal, Anne Hathaway, Michelle Williams and Randy Quaid.

These are the only two movies that come to mind. Certainly, if you look at the actors involved in the projects, there are some big names in there. For the same- sex marriage fight, just like the interracial marriages fight before it, the use of these big-name Hollywood actors gave them strong credibility and ammo, as this indicated that these sorts of celebrities supported the movements.

The next thing we will look at is the impact in network television as we did with interracial marriages. When we think about how the media embraces gays and lesbians on TV, we can see a stronghold on popular culture. To the best of my knowledge, I remember *Will and Grace* as the first time I witnessed this on TV. Again, I'm not stating a fact here as I am sure there were others, but this is the first one that I remember off hand, or at least, it is the first to come to mind.

We fast forward to 2015 and if we look at the trend, we start to come up with all kinds of examples of this. There is a large list of television shows to choose from with at least one gay or lesbian character. There is *Modern Family*, *Madam Secretary*, *Gotham*, and *Empire*, just to name a few. Pretty mainstream huh? Well there's more. Gays and lesbians even have their own networks and channels like The Logo Channel. Based on the media fact along, what makes you think that same sex marriage won't be legalized soon in every state.

So by this you are probably thinking, it would never happen, because 10 is a small number compared to 52 and some others of you may be even thinking if it did happen we are light years away from that huh? Well, what if I told you, we may be a lot closer than you think. You see just like the interracial movement, it only took a few instances, situations, and states to get the ball rolling, and others, due to the massive number of people supporting the movement in their home states, people like Governors, Mayors, Congressman, and Senators, are going have to get on board soon if they want to keep their jobs and keep their approval ratings high. Remember, numbers control politics, politics control politicians, politicians control laws, and laws control people.

Here is the thing, over 30 plus years ago, a Senator, Governor, Congressman, Mayor, or even a President didn't have to worry about pleasing gays and lesbians because the number of supporters were just too small. And the number of active gays and lesbians (out of the closest) were far and between. But if you look around now, you can't sit hear and read this and think that you don't know at least a handful of gay or lesbian people, Also, you may even be of some kind of religious faith that tells you that this is unnatural behavior, but due to the fact that you know some of these people or have some kind of a connection to them, you have sympathy, then your natural response would be to support them especially if you have a family member that's in this fight, even if it's something that you don't condone.

Strange huh? Sick Huh? Unbelievable Huh? Twisted Huh? Well, here we go again with those terms. You see when you get to the point of accepting something that years ago you could never envision accepting, and you see more and more masses of people doing it, you brain meter that used those phrases in the past like strange, twisted, sick, and unbelievable starts to mild down. Once this happens, you start to reason with yourself and think things like, well they aren't hurting anyone, so I guess it's cool, I won't ever do it that's unnatural but it seems that thousands upon thousands of people are doing it now, so it can't be all that bad. This is what leads to acceptance, this is what makes us more liberal, when we clearly had a strong stance against certain things in the pasts. Ironically, when it comes to this issue (the issue of same sex marriages) we as average Americans don't even have the biggest problem. Christian preachers do.

Well what if you are a Christian Minster? Then what? Will you let them in your church? Will you marry them? If they are in large numbers in your church, do you clearly speak against this type of behavior like the Bible says and loose members? It's a pure catch 22 and I may be able to shed some light on this. Let's use another example as we look back to an issue in the 1920's.

In the 1920's, years after lawmakers cracked down on the Klu Klux Klan and just about des-banned down to just a few thousand, the Klan felt they needed to get their numbers, power and control back up. So instead of just aiming hatred toward African Americans, they included Catholics, Jews and even immigrants. The Klan at this time was led by William Joseph

Simmons. This was a result of changes in traditional American Society. Most churches had several active members of the Klan in their congregations and did not want to lose those members. At this time, the Klan members in churches now started going to the Christian Ministers who in-turn convinced the rest of their congregations to support the Klan and also convinced their members that the Klan was not as portrayed by the media and Conservative America.

This was a tactic that paid off and actually got the Klan's numbers to the millions. They even marched on Washington later that decade. The reason why I brought this up is to show you how tactics are used to sway anyone, even

Christian Ministers to take a position that is clearly against what the Bible teaches.

So now as we see, due to the emergence of homosexuals flooding churches and filling the collection plates, some preachers are getting on board and coming out in support of this using the tactic of only God can judge and that this is clearly not spelled out in the Bible and also if it is, then it is old testament teachers which of course some deem as not parallel to modern times as Jesus came fourth and changed the old laws. It's a tactic that's similar in content to the 1920's Klan example. One such example is in the Presbyterian Church in Wisconsin ordaining the first openly gay preacher, Rev. Scott Anderson in 2011. This is clearly a tactic that let gays and lesbians know that the church is clearly starting to get behind their movement and may even be interpreting scripture differently now, or perhaps since we all interpret scripture differently, maybe it can be condoned. I'm not taking a side on this issue. I'm simply making a point here. This is an invitation if you will, for homosexuals to join the faith and to come openly to their place of worship. Some are even performing marriages for same sex couples. You also have many of these preachers that won't speak out against such behavior because there are just too many in their congregation, or they just don't want to offend supporters of same sex marriages in their church.

Now there are some that take a strong stance against this and speak on it often, and don't have a problem stating scripture as it is written and interpreting scripture as it is written. One such man who happens to be one of my favorite pastors is Fred Price Jr, the son of Doctor Fred Price Senior. This is a man in which I got some insight and influence for this book.

In his lesson entitled The Pursuit of Holiness, Fred Price Jr, states that "men laying with men and women laying with women is an abomination to the Lord". He quotes scripture when he speaks on this in the lesson called "The Pursuit of Holiness". In Leviticus 18:23 it states "you shall not lie with a male as with a women, it is an abomination". Fred Price Jr has stayed true to scripture and to himself. He even speaks about some other unnatural behaviors in the same series of lessons such as bestiality and necrophilia. He says that these things are detestable and that they sicken the Lord. These behaviors are a stench to the Lord's nostrils. He goes on to quote many scriptures supporting his teachings including Job 4, Isaiah 34, and the book of Galatians.

While Pastor Price continues to teach Bible principles and what is truly in his heart, there are other preachers, who will remain nameless, that are accepting unnatural homosexual behavior. They even allow homosexuals to marry in their places of worship. Then there are others who take a more subtle approach. They do not speak badly about homosexuality but they will offer prayers and some support without taking a harsh stance against them, like Joel Osteen. Now by no means am I attacking him or Fred Price Jr for any of their approaches. I understand it is a catch 22. So as a Christian, it is difficult to deal with the issue of homosexuality and I think these two have found the best way for them individually to deal with this lifestyle. Others, however, it seem have deviated from even dealing with this issue or speaking on it. This may just be a direct result of those in support of same sex marriages or activities being major contributors to their collection plates.

There are currently 5 states where gay and lesbian marriages are legal and they are as follows:

Massachusetts

Connecticut

Iowa-(1st state in the mid-west)

Vermont

New Hampshire-(5th state bill signed by Governor John Lynch)

Now you might say that this is a small number of states and due other states fighting against same sex marriages that it may not go any further, but if you truly believe that then I'll tell you the one about Santa Claus, the Tooth Fairly, and the Easter Bunny. And if you believe in those, then maybe you believe that it won't go much further. But remember, it started small with interracial marriages (just a few states) and then it grew into 50 states in a very short period of time. I'm even sure that perhaps, it may legal in a few more states by the time this book is published.

Are you starting to see the correlation? It is my theory, that in about 3-5 more years, in about 2020, same sex marriages will be legal in every state in the Union. Mark my words, in 2020, you will all say Michael you were right and then we move on to the next fight.

This is where we are now, and this is also where we thought we would never be, but here we are knocking on the doorstep of having same sex marriages legal in every state.

Now if your grandparents are still alive, even your parents, put the book down for a second and go ask them how they felt about this issue 30 to 40 years ago. I'll wait.... Did you do it? Great! And I can tell you exactly what they said. I bet, watch this, and I quote, "well son or daughter, 30 plus years ago if you would have told me that we would now be on the verge of same sex marriages being legalized, I would have said Strange? Sick? Unbelievable? Twisted? Sounds familiar? Yea, your great grandparents probably said the same thing about 60 plus years ago about interracial marriages.

Gays and lesbians are coming out in larger and larger numbers and in this country, numbers control politics, politics control politicians, politicians control laws, and laws control people.

If the previous statement is true, and we know this by history, then we can rest assure that the numbers are in favor of those in the current fight (same sex marriages). Thus, same sex marriages will eventually pass in every state because there are millions upon millions of gays and lesbians coming out every day in America and unless this changes - meaning those numbers decline (which they probably won't), we won't be able to do anything to stop this.

Another interesting thing that Fred Price Jr spoke about was that in the days of Noah, before the great flood, 'the normal was abnormal and the abnormal was normal". Just think about that as we will re-visit this in a later chapter.

NEW LAW – ALL STATES

Well on June 26, 2015, "In a long-sought victory for the gay rights movement, the Supreme Court ruled by a 5-to-4 vote...that the Constitution guarantees a right to same-sex marriage."

This information was something I added after my final editing.

So where are we going? We now know where we have been and we even know where we are.

Who's on deck?

Who will be the next group to pick up the touch and start the next fight?

Who is in the closet now and lingering in the woodwork's waiting to take a stand?

Who is paying attention to the same sex rights movement and now wants their turn?

Well, my guess would be the polygamist.

POLYGAMY

Often referred to as Consensual Non-Monogamy, polygamy is the marriage which includes two or more partners. When a woman is married to two or more husbands it is called polyandry. Polygamy is when a man is married to more than one wife at a time. The fight for legalized polygamy has probably been around just as long as interracial marriages and same sex marriage. For some reason, the numbers have always been quite low, so there has not been an outpouring of protest or major attempts to get it legalized. Now in saying that, these numbers of those in favor of polygamy have been low, but that's not to say that a massive number of Americans wouldn't like to see it legalized and even in some ways wish they could be open and have several spouses to accommodate multiple needs. But most Americans, just will not admit it, perhaps fearing the outrage and response they are going to receive from their significant other.

Here is my theory. Follow me on this.

There has always got to be a reason or excuse to start a fight or protest. It has to be something symbolic. Though for some of you reading this are on the opposite side of the fence, including myself on most of these issues, it is symbolic to those who want these rights. Having the right to do what is generally considered to be unnatural and unacceptable behavior is symbolic.

Before I get into my theory, let's take a look at these statistics on infidelity, courtesy of InfidelityFacts.com. Then I will explain after we review these stats.

- The percentage of marriages in which one or both of the spouses admit physical or emotional infidelity is 41%
- Marriages that end in divorce in America is 53%
- 3% of "arranged marriages" (those marriages where parents pick the child's spouses) end in divorce
- Even after an affair has been discovered or admitted to 31% of the marriages last.
- 36% of women and men admit to infidelity on a business trip

- The highest divorce rate in medical fields are marriage counselors and psychiatrists

- 68% of women say they would have an affair if they were certain that they would not get caught: 74%

- 54% of women admit committing infidelity in any relationship

- Percentage of men and women who admit to having an affair with a co-worker: 36%

- 17% of women and men admit to infidelity (physical or emotional) with a sister-in-law or brother-in-law

- 74% of men say they would have an affair if they were certain that they would not get caught:

Michael Walker

InfidelityFacts.com http://www.infidelityfacts.com/index.html 2006

Now if we look at these statistics we will see that 41% of those marriages that end in divorce are due to infidelity. That's a large percentage. So where are we going? Keep in mind that every fight has a starting point. Remember in the introduction I spoke about how and why the necrophilia fight began and their reasoning to pass their laws? Well here is where some polygamist may derive their reasoning for the fight to make polygamy legal.

You see, one theory of mine, is that due to infidelity the divorce rate is so high- 41%. Polygamist will go on record as saying that if you let them marry multiple partners, then there would be no reason for divorce. In other words, the divorce rate would go down substantially. Think about it, this is strong ammo for them and they may have a valid point here after all, why would anyone get divorced if they can 'have their cake and eat it too'. Now, in saying that, the ammo we could use is from research that shows mormon divorce rates appear to be no more different than the average American divorce rate but that doesn't mean that they will not use the infidelity rate stats to boost and support their fight.

So the basic meaning here is the more spouses you have, then the more likely you would not go out and cheat, and when you think about it, it makes sense that this could be a valid point by them, because let's face it, if a man or women has multiple spouses of different criteria, supplying everything they need, then it would be no need to cheat. They can simply go from one room to the next.

So we fast forward to about 2025 which is right about the time when the same sex marriage fight comes to an end because right around 2023, it too becomes legal in every state.

And here comes the polygamists whose numbers have multiplied into the hundreds of thousands. As they march on Washington with their picket signs and demand the opportunity to marry as many people as they so desire, they are saying things in the media like, well if people of different races, religions, and creeds can get married, and if people of the same sex can get married, then we should be able to marry as many partners as we would like.

They would probably go on to say, We are not hurting anyone, we just want our rights, just as the interracial couples, and gays and lesbians have stated before in previous chapters.

Like I said this fight has been around for a while but not massive in numbers. However, watch as the year's progress how those numbers will multiply.

Strange huh? Twisted huh? Unbelievable huh? Sick huh? Well, not if you pay attention. Before we get into where we are going with this, let's take a look at how this whole polygamy thing got started.

Polygamy means the state of marriage to many spouses or Consensual Non-Monogamy. Polygamy in the United States probably has been around a long time, but as far as we know it wasn't any real strong movement until the movement got started by Joseph Smith, the founder of the Latter Day Saints on July 12, 1843. Other leaders included Brigham Young and Herbert Kimball. All three men took several plural wives.

After Smith's death in 1844, Young felt that the church was secure enough to openly practice polygamy to the rest of the world. It was in 1852, about the time that the government threatened to take legal action against the church. So let's look at the previous statement. The government always takes action against an unnatural behavior when it starts because the number of people participating is simply too low. There is not a reason to accommodate those involved because the majority of those around when an unnatural behavior starts are totally against the behavior. But keep in mind we are in a majority rules nation. And after the polygamist see they we have legalized gay and lesbian marriages, you can bet that they are going have a lot to say about that in conjunction with their fight. And their numbers will start increasing dramatically as well. Think about it, if the constitution says that a marriage in this country is a union between a man and a women, and we allow gays and lesbians to marry, then we break that once, and we'll have to break it again. I can promise you that this will be their argument and I can even see it as being a loophole in other so called unnatural behaviors, and believe me, if we make an exception for one, then we are going to find ourselves making many more. Give it time.

"In 1882, the United States Congress passed the Edmunds Act, which made polygamy a felony". Hundreds of Mormon men and women were arrested. So the church then decided to ban the practice of polygamy on September 25, 1890.

Thereafter and into today, there are several sects that openly practice or support polygamy. These sects are called The Fundamentalist Church of Jesus Christ of Latter Day Saints, The Latter Day Church of Christ, and The Apostolic United Brethren. These groups are currently active in Utah, Arizona, Colorado, and even in Canada. In Utah, there are about 40,000 Mormon Fundamentalists.

Another fact would be that there are only about 15,000 more people with no church affiliation practicing polygamy.

Those may be small numbers you might say and at this stage you are absolutely right. But keep in mind we are at least 10 plus years from this fight. Also keep in mind that we are still in the same sex marriage fight. So these numbers can and will increase. Some will even use the current fight of same sex marriages as a basses to marry multiple partners. And I'm not just taking about men. Yes, I am speaking about women as well. Now you might think that men only are interested in marrying multiple partners due to the current state of the Mormon church but remember, when one starts fighting for their rights, others will follow suit. This is the correlation. This fight might clearly be designed for men wanting multiple partners and wives, but women will want and desire more partners and husbands as well. This falls along the lines of serial monogamy or frequent marriage if you will which is a form of polygamy. If fact, most who practice polygamy tend to practice serial monogamy.

Strange huh? Twisted huh? Sick huh? Unbelievable huh? Well, I think we've been here before in previous chapters and it gets more intense by the minute.

All I can ask at this point is "What would possibly make you think that polygamists will not enter the fight soon? Because when you think about it, polygamists will have some religious basis for their beliefs, whereas gays, lesbians, and even interracial couples will not?" What I mean by that is that Mormons now use the 1886 revelation to John Taylor as their basis.

John Taylor was the third leader of The Church of Jesus Christ of Latter Day Saints. The 1886 Revelation was a so called divine text that he claimed to receive basically stating to re-instate earlier founding principles.

Other religious values and excuses or reasoning for this would be the Biblical great King Solomon, who had hundreds of wives. Some will definitely use this as a reasoning tool because he was the wisest king to ever live. After all, if the wisest king that ever lived had hundreds of wives, then surely some will say we should follow in his footsteps. Using the Bible and twisting its meaning and substance

65

to your own sick needs is a common practice. Slave owners did this with slaves back in the early 1800's. The premise was using the verse on slaves to obey their masters and also using scriptures on giving slaves lashes, and other scriptures on Noah's son who was cursed to being a servant of others as being a man of color. It wasn't right then and of course it is not right now. But I'm sure in about 10 years, if the fight is pretty strong, maybe my mind would even change as so would yours.

We see these things from afar and use the terms twisted, sick, unnatural, and unacceptable because it is not yet massive enough to change our minds. We were all brought up a certain way, but think about it. How many of you have changed your mindset to accept same sex marriages or even interracial marriages? Well, maybe many of you. Remember what I said numbers control politics, politics control politicians, politicians control laws, and laws control people. So what makes you think that you won't change your mind about polygamy in about 10 to 15 years as you see hundreds of thousands protesting and raising awareness on this subject.

The current state of polygamy is primary [arranged marriages between younger women, sometimes teenagers and older men]. This was a concept that started to raise eyebrows when the FBI'S 10 most wanted list Mormon leader, Warren Jeffs took over.

Warren Jeffs was born December 3rd, 1955 and was name as the leader or prophet of

Fundamentalist Church of Jesus Christ of Latter-Day Saints. He was preceded by his father Rulon Jeffs who passed in 2002. Just a week after his father's death he married all but two of his father's wives. His father just like him, also practice polygamy. Warren Jeffs made himself the only person in the church able to perform marriages. He assigned wives to husbands. Jeffs started arranging marriages between older men and teenage girls including himself. The net worth of his ministry was well over $100 million, which included lots of land in several states. Jeffs was arrested in 2006 for sexually assulting children.

Let me state it briefly another way so you can see where I'm going with this, the current state of polygamy entails [younger women being forced to marry older men]. Now this is not what polygamy is defined as but it is the current state of it. So where will that lead us? Where are we going? When will it stop? Keep in mind that one fight always lead to another. In saying that and looking at the bold statements above guess who's up next?

Well, think about it for a second? Things progress from bad to worse as the years go by. Now we get into the really twisted and sick.

First up Child Molesters.

CHILD MOLESTERS OR ADULT/CHILD SEX

Well people, the year in 2045ish and the USA is changing for the worse. Things have gotten so out of hand, that we can't seem to get a handle on anything. A few years back we passed laws legalizing polygamy in all 52 states in the union and now the sick and really twisted start to come out. There numbers were small, at least as far as we know, right around the time I wrote this book. But prisons were filled with them and we even had them register as sex offenders so that everyone could know how sick they were or are. They have been through Chris Hansen, dateline NBC, embarrassed, arrested, and some even put to death. But here they are, as strong as they have ever been and in large numbers. They are marching on Washington, just like prior groups before them, groups like interracial couples, gays, lesbians, and polygamists.

This is truly a sad day in America as we watch them and their supporters on the news with their Pickett signs and bullhorns causing riots and outburst. They are making statements to the news media saying things like, if gays, lesbians, polygamist and interracial couples can marry or have sex, then why can't we have sex with children or minors. They are making other familiar comments like "we are not hurting anyone, we just want our rights". Remember that saying? Well again we hear it, and this time we get sicker to our stomachs, but wait, weren't we sick to our stomachs 10, 20, 30, 40, or even 60 years ago before some of the other things in previous chapters became legal? Remember? yea we were, and then as we got more and more liberal and tolerant to others views and feelings, we toned it down.

So will we tone this down? My thoughts are that if you are reading this book, it sickens you that I would even suggest such a thing as us toning this one down, but most of us may not even be around then when this comes full circle. Better yet, it may be sooner then what we think. Remember, each generation gets more and more liberal and tolerant of unnatural behavior. We did. So why would our children or grandchildren not be liberal enough to tolerate this type of behavior. It will be a different time. We are talking in the future some 40 or more years, at least, we hope it is far out. I can't tell you exactly when it is coming but I can tell you for sure that it is coming.

Let's look back on the last bold statement in the previous chapter. Remember what I said about the current state of polygamy? It usually involves younger women being forced to marry older men. This could very well be the trigger, or at least one of the triggers, to try and legalize child and adult marriages, as well as child and adult sexual relationships.

Really strange huh? Really twisted huh? Really unbelievable huh? Really sick huh? I could not agree with you more, yes it is. So where are we going? How will we get there? Where are we at present with this? I'm going to share with you some things that clearly show we are on our way to this fight and when we get there, it's really going to start a chain reaction toward the truly sick and twisted.

I'm going to go in three segments here, so let's review them before I get into details.

Segment 1-History of child molesters or adults/child sex to the present

Segment 2- Present fights for child molestation or adults/child sex

Segment 3-The future fight for child molestation or adults/child sex to be legalized

Let's start with the 1st segment.

The issues of child molestation became public in the 1970's and 1980's. In the 1920's, with all that was going on then, it was virtually non-existent. National estimates on this trend started in 1948, however; the trend itself can be traced back to 1857 in France where the first recorded reports surfaced.

Before the 1970's, those who participated in child molestation and/or adults/child sex activities were primarily in secrecy and small in numbers. Let's look at this. Like groups before in previous chapters we talked about trends taking place in secrecy and small numbers. Can you see the correlation here? Like interracial marriages, same sex marriages and polygamy, the trend was slow starting and the numbers were few. So in previous years, there was no need to address the issues of child molestation.

Around the late 1960's states started to enact laws to combat sexual child abuse and child molestation. Here is another correlation. If you look at this trend, you will notice that the 1960's seemed to be a common period for massive numbers of people participating in unnatural behaviors, or at least the un-natural behaviors we talked about thus far.

We fast forward to 1974, and find where Congress passed the Child Abuse Prevention and Treatment Act. This was one of the first laws aimed at prosecuting this type of behavior. Also, in 1979, the National Abuse Coalition pushed harder to have Congress to pass many more laws.

In 1986, Congress passed Child Abusive Victims Right Act which gives children who have been sexually abused civil claims against their accusers.

So we see, in the 1980's and 1990's, there were finally laws to prosecute child abusers.

This is a brief history of child sexual abuse and child sexual abuse laws in the Unites States. So where are we going with this? Well, let's get into segment 2.

So where are we now with this? Well, remember that every unnatural behavior has to have a reason behind the fight, or at least a reason in the mind of the person or persons who participate in a particular behavior. What could possibly be the reason for marriage between and adult and a child? One theory of mine is that teens nowadays are more subject to manipulation from adults. Adults tend to manipulate the minds of children and teens persuading them to conform to a certain way of life. We then see the children or teens who have been manipulated demanding or asking for what they themselves have conformed to. This is likely to happen in the future. Instead of adults leading this fight, it may very well be a fight lead by younger boys and girls. Children and teens are becoming more and more susceptible to brain washing every day. I am not sure we have what it takes to reverse this.

If we look around now, we see over the past 20 years, several cases of adults wanting to marry or have sexual relationships with children and if it were legal, they would marry children. We may think this is years out, but actually they've already begun this fight. They are prepping for this future fight already. Adults are having real and sexual relationships with children in massive numbers in this current era. These adults are being prosecuted but in spite of this, their numbers are rapidly growing.

There are two groups that I want to focus on here, teachers and church leaders. Those two categories typically have the most influence over children.

Teachers:

Here are just a few examples of teachers having sexual relationships with children.

- In August of 1998, in California, a teacher was accused of having sex with a 14 year old babysitter.
- In March of 2000, a substitute teacher, in California, was accused of having sex with multiple teenage students.

- In November of 2004, in California as well, an ex-principal faceds charges of child pornography.
- In Delaware, in March of 2007, a teacher was sentenced for an affair with a teenage student.
- In South Carolina, January 2005, a teacher was convicted of sex with a minor.
- In Kentucky, in May 2007, a teacher admits to having sex with a young boy.

These are just a few examples of how teachers, whom we trust with our children, are betraying us in the worst way.

Spiritual leaders:

This next set of examples is of our spiritual leaders betraying us in the same way:

- In Florida, February 1996, a youth minister molested a dozen teenage boys.

- In November of 1996, the Mormon sex scandals in Utah came to public attention. This was when multiple Mormon leaders prosecuted for having sex with and marrying underage girls.

- In Missouri, October 1998, Reverend Gregory Robertson, 40 years of age, was charged with the rape of three teenage girls.

- In New Jersey, August of 1999, a Salvation Army minister had to register as a sex offender.

- In California, June of 2001, an ex-pastor was suspected of molesting two boys.

- In January of 2003, nationwide, rampant sex abuse was found by many priests.

- In Virginia, May of 2009, a former church leader pleads guilty to child molestation sex crimes.

These are just a few examples of some of the betrayal that we've encountered. You can get a feel of how massive the numbers are currently. If we examine this, 30 years ago, those numbers were a lot lower. Now in comparison to previous chapters, those numbers too were low 30 plus years ago prior to their time. If those numbers increased dramatically over the past 30 years, what makes you think that those numbers will not triple or even quadruple over the next 30 plus years. Where are we going with this?

Currently, the fight is stalled. This does not mean that those in support of child/adult marriages or child/adult sexual relationships are not fighting for their rights as we speak.

- Mary Letuuraneaur, who molested a 12 year old boy, married the boy in 2005 when he was at the legal age of 18.
- In 2013, Leah Shipmen, age 42, an ex-teacher married a student that she was accused of molesting when he was 15 years old.
- In 2013, Kimberly Bynum, age 29, had sex with a 17 year old minor, then married him to avoid prosecution.

These are just a few examples of those in the current fight. There are others not mentioned in this book. It is true we have guys like Steve Wilkos who stand up against these monsters, but there are just not enough people like him. We do applaud and support his efforts.

Segment three gets into where we will go with this. Look at it realistically. Only time will tell, but as more and more adults molest children, and more and more children marry adults who have molested them, it will become more normal. Remember what was mentioned in a previous chapter about what I said Fred Price Jr talked about. In the days of Noah, the normal was abnormal and then because the normal, same here. In the end times christians like Fred Price Jr believes that that abnormal behavior will become normal so our children's children or great grandchildren will see this trend as acceptable behavior.

You may say the numbers are not there now? However, you have to admit that those numbers are increasing daily. Twenty years ago, there was no need for Chris Hanson, dateline NBC, or Steve Wilkos. The reason being is because there was not enough reported or recorded cases to start a fight against them. Now even law enforcement has task forces to crack down on this type of behavior but they too are overwhelmed.

Can you hear them people? Can you see them with their picket signs and their bullhorns in 2045 saying things like "We are not hurting anyone, we just want our rights". I can. I can also hear them saying things like, "that young girl or boy wants to marry me and they are old enough to make their own decisions" though they are clearly not mature or old enough to marry. To add to this, I'm sure they'll also say, "If interracial couples, gay and lesbian couples, and polygamists can do it, then why can't we?" Trust me people, this will in turn open doors we never thought possible in this country.

Another important thing to remember about child/adult sexual relationships or marriage's, is that a large majority of these relationships come from within the family structure. In other words, most child molesters are molesting family members.

You may still be in denial. You may even say that the buck may stop with polygamy. Again, it was supposed to stop with interracial marriages and it didn't. Then gay and lesbian marriage's but it didn't.

Even if you are a politician reading this, you may now say that you would never vote on any law supporting these rights. Let's look back on what I said in previous chapters. Numbers control politics, politics control politicians, politicians control laws, and laws control people. So in reading this again, if the majority of people support this lifestyle or who will be doing this in future years, what makes you think any politician will not support it? Most politicians want to keep their jobs. Of course, once they do vote to legalize child/adult marriages, then that's where the rationalizing will begin. Remember this all too familiar sentence? "Well I don't do it, and my kids or family members don't do it, and they are not hurting anyone. So if it will stop child molestation or child abuse, then we should pass the law. It is the right thing to do". On that note, I think you get the point thus far. I think you understand that there is a real and present dangerous possibility that some 30 or more years from now, adult/child marriages and sexual relationships will be legal.

Strange huh? Twisted huh? Unbelievable huh? Sick huh? I agree. Prepare yourself because it is coming.

So where are we going? We now know where we were, where we been and where we are headed next as well as what is to come.

Whose turn is it next?

Who is ready to pick up the fight after things get really twisted as child molesters get their rights and laws passed to protect them? I would have to say it will be those who want to marry their own family members. That is those prone to incest and incestuous relationships.

INCEST

The year is 2055ish, and we are at a place of no return. Child molesters scored a major victory some 10 years prior. We, in this nation, have become so open that we have very limited control over what goes on anymore. In front of the White House, as well as, on Capitol Hill is where they gather. There will be brothers, sisters, cousins, aunts, uncles, nieces, nephews, moms, and dads. The signs are out and the bull horn is loud. Their chants are loud and they are using familiar phrases like "We just want our rights, we are not hurting anyone". Other phases include, "If I want to have sex and marry my own child or niece, nephew or cousin, that's my business". They go on to proclaim that since in our nation we permits interracial couples get married, and allow gays and lesbians get married, and license polygamists to marry multiple wives or husbands, then opening the door to incest and incestuous relationships is only fair. They rationalize that our nation even endorses child molesters to marry children and then question, "Why can we not marry our own brothers, sisters, moms, or dads, etc.

This is a direct result of the changing times. Congress has to make a decision quickly on this. Certainly it will be easier for them now since they passed the law allowing children to marry or have sexual relationships with adults. So where are we going? Consider the following facts.

Incest is a relationship between family members or close relatives. Incest usually involves a relationship between an adult and child which is a form of child abuse.

In ancient times, some cultures around the world embraced incest, such as in ancient Egypt, and ancient Greece. Tutankhamun and his half-sister Ankhesermaun were married for example. In ancient Greece Spartan King Leonidas I, married his niece, Gorgo. These are just two examples of incestuous marriages but there are many more.

As by now we know that those on the picket lines will be using phrases like we are not hurting anyone, we just want our rights. But in truth just like child/adult marriages they are indeed hurting people. One of the main problems with incestuous relationships is inbreeding. Inbreeding causes the children of these relationships to become more susceptible to sicknesses, diseases and birth disorders. So those of us that are looking to fight against getting legislation passed in reference to this do have some ammunition. The question is, "Is it enough? I would imagine when this time comes, and the numbers are so high of those participating in this incestuous lifestyle, or those in support of it will have numbers on their side. Getting back to my theory that 'numbers control politics, politics control politicians, politicians control laws, and laws control people'. We know that we may be fighting a losing battle.

One of the points we talked about in previous chapters was that every fight has a trigger. Each trigger usually stems from a previous fight. If we look at the previous chapters, the fight for adult/child marriages or sexual relationships could very well stem the fight for incest. My theory is that some of those adults who are abusing teens and children, manipulating their minds to control and marry them, may also be controlling some of their own family members. This is another form of child sexual abuse. In most cases it usually involves guardians of the abusers or cousins, aunts and uncles and even in some case grandparents and parents. Here are a few examples of this:

A Melbourne doctor is expected to soon learn his professional fate for having a four-year incestuous relationship with his daughter, which produced a son

Mistie Atkinson, 32, tracked down her estranged 16-year-old son. The two were found in a hotel room on March 2nd engaged in incestuous activity. Police found nude photographs of the mother on the boy's cell phone, including photos of her performing oral sex on him.

A Montgomery County woman who was arrested for shoplifting and made headlines after deputies found her kissing her brother through the jail cell bars

These are just a few examples of insestual behavior and believe me, there are probably countless others that are just not being reported now and I believe that the reason for them not being reported is due to the shame it causes the family and right-fully so. I also believe it can also be due to those avoiding prosecution. But let's examine it for a second. We talked about how marriage is listed in the constitution as one man and one woman and then we turn around and allow laws to pass allowing same sex marriages. This is clearly a conflict, anyone in any of these fights can make the same case as same sex couples did. Some even say that the courts would need to decide how this in the constitution can be interpreted but it clearly states that *marriage as a union between one man and one woman. It doesn't say a child and adult, it doesn't say same sex, and it doesn't say humans and animals. But if you look at that statement literally, then those who want to marry within their own family, have a clear upper hand on this one because one man and one women could be in the same family. So when their fight comes up, guess what they will use as ammo? You guessed it, the one man, one woman union.*

Another aspect of this fight would be to use the Bible as grounds to stand on, remember if Adam and Eve were the only two people on the planet, then how on earth, did we get here. if you believe the Bible. You guessed it, insest. Here me out here, if the Bible is true and it says Adam and eve had other sons and daughters besides Cain and Abel, then the only way to be fruitful and multiply the earth as stated in the book on Genesis, would be for the sons and daughters to marry each other. This gives those who participate in incest and want to marry a family member another form of ammo to further and continue their fight. Remember, we talked about this earlier with slave owners using the Bible to fulfil their own twisted needs. Well, this is certainly usable as well.

Father daughter relationships are among the most common of these. So in saying that, you can believe that child abusers from within families will step up to this fight.

Sure, there will probably be cousins and uncles and even sisters and brothers coming forth for the fight to legalize incestuous relationships. I believe that the majority of those fighting this fight, will be adults who have molested their own children or family members that they have been left in charge of or responsible for.

This is a direct result of how far things will go. Some of you reading this may not think it is possible but if adult/child marriages and polygamy get legalized, this is just another step to 'liberate' us and give everyone 'their rights'. Yes, there are some sick and twisted people out here but sick and twisted people are sick and twisted in different ways.

You see, some like children, some like multiple marriages at the same time, and others may like their own family members. It sounds very strange and twisted to me and maybe to you. To our ancestors, our parents and grandparents, interracial marriages sounded strange and twisted. But look where we are now with that. To some of us same sex marriages sounds strange, sick, and twisted. Again, look at where we are now with that. This is the true circle of unnatural behavior. It will go on and on to the point where every twisted group would feel that in a free country, they should have the 'rights' to exercise and live in their own twisted sick idea of freedom and rights. Like you and I, they feel that they should have the right to do what they want to do, regardless of how sick and twisted it is.

Another aspect of this fight, just like all other fights that preceded it, is the power and influence of media, the BIG SCREEN. Well, there is one such movie that addresses this issue and that was the movie Flowers in the Attic. This movie was directed by Jeffrey Bloom starring Louise Fletcher, Victoria Tennant, Kristy Swanson, and Jeb Stuart Adams. This movie came out in 1987 and was remade in 2014. It depicts a brother and sister whose mom locked them in an attic at her father's house as he was dying. She wanted to make certain to inherent his fortune. The father was not aware that she had children and if he found out, then it would ruin the inheritance for her. The siblings bonded. They had a sexual relationship and became lovers. Although the movie was not received very well back in the 1980's Flowers in the Attic was, however, received well in 2014 as I understand. A mini-series is being made out of it.

This goes back to what I was saying about the media and big screen embracing a concept that may not have been popular or accepted at some point. Flowers in the Attic, a movie about an incestuous relationship was not acceptable in 1980's but was embraced in 2014, a later point in history. We see in this example, the movie and book turned heads and was forbidden and highly unacceptable 20 plus years ago to coming to a point of preparing for this as it was re-made in 2014.

So as this fight goes before lawmakers, guess what happens? Well, you guessed right, it passed and now there is a bill on the books to legalize incest and incestuous relationships. It is not hard to imagine. We have already crossed the threshold with adult/child relationships.

Really, really strange huh? Really, really twisted huh? Really, really unbelievable huh? Well, at this point, no not really. I guess it is time to move on to the next fight.

Who's on deck?

Who has watched the incestuous fight and is waiting their turn. Whose numbers are increasing dramatically? Who can't wait to get lawmakers talking about them?

We can only imagine. We have already explored the extreme human sexual perversions and some of you may even be thinking it can't get any worse than that. But can it? Welcome to the extreme twisted section, not that some other chapters were not but the next two are beyond your wildest imagination. We'll start with Zoophilia and Bestiality.

ZOOPHILIA AND BESTIALITY

We'll people, the year is 2070ish and it looks as if we have lost our way. Things are so out of control that we have in recent years legalized incest and child/adult marriage. We are so liberal and open to the feelings and rights of others that we let things that we deem as unnatural at some point in time, become commonplace. So why would we not legalize zoophilia and bestiality? If we have gone as far as legalizing some of the other unnatural behaviors, then why on earth should we deny these sick and twisted individuals their rights?

When they hit Capitol Hill, you better believe that they will be using the same phrases like "We are not hurting anyone, we just want our rights". They would also be saying things like, "You let gays, lesbians, interracial couples, child molesters, polygamists and those in incestuous relationships get married or have sexual relationships, so why can't we?" Do you hear them people? I do. And guess what, ironically, they will have a symbolic point. Who is to say, at this point, that their rights are not just as important and valid as those of the other unnatural behaviors?

What will we do and where are we going? Where are we now with this? Where have we been with this? Who, currently, is fighting zoophilia and beastiality? Let's take a look shall we.

Zoophilia is a sexual fixation with animals. Bestiality is sexual activity between human and animals. The two terms are somewhat interchangeable. Zoophilia refers to fixation (wanting to see or imagining but maybe not acting on it).

Beastiality refers to the act of a human having sexual relations with an animal.

Reports show the percentage of people who had sexual contact with animals at one point in their lives as 8% for men and 3.6% for women. This is a staggering statistic. That is 8% for men and 3.6% for women. So with a stat like that, this tells you that this is a serious problem in our society today. This is a dilemma that needs to be addressed seriously. Now imagine if those numbers increase, and history and time tells us it will. Remember in previous chapters, those numbers were very low at some point but as time progressed, major increases took place. Also, if you look at those stats that I just mentioned, I'm sure those numbers were a lot lower 20 plus years ago. Pay attention as those numbers increase over time, just like the others.

Most of these cases are reported and confined to those living on farms, which would give some explanation on why it is happening. This does not change the fact that it is happening on and off the farm.

There are several forms of Zoophiliac behaviors or manifestations and they are as follows:

- Human Animal role Players-those who role play with animals
- Romantic Zoophiles-those who aspire a a romantic encounter with animals
- Zoophilic Fatisizers-those who fantisize about being with animals
- Sadistic Bestials-those who delight in this behavior due to cults and satanic worship
- Fetishitic Zoophilia-Practiced by those who have an animal fetish.
- Opportunistic Zoophiles-Those who will jump at any chance to have a sexual relationship with animals at any given time.

- Exclusive Zoophiles-Those who are only exclusive sexually with a specific animal or pet.

Studies show that those who practice zoophilia, may do so due to a lack of childhood experimentation and abuse. This may cause those individuals to act out and seek sexual relationships with species other than human. These individuals will not seek help for this condition, so it can be difficult to recognize.

Further research includes that some who practice zoophilia become aroused by only certain animals while others can become aroused by multiple or several species of animals. Many of these individuals are not attracted to humans at all.

From a historical and cultural standpoint, there are also instances of this type of behavior referred to in the Bible. In Leviticus 18:23 it reads "And you shall not lay with any beast and defile yourself with it, neither shall any women give herself to a beast to lie with it: it is a perversion." Now let's look at this verse for a second. In the same chapter we talked earlier about how this verse also speaks about homosexual activities. We realize that over time those who are homosexual, may feel that the scripture can be interpreted differently and may even use the scripture to push their own agenda in a different way. We can see clearly from the verse that this is forbidden. Yet over time some kind of way, we find a way to counter or justify unnatural behavior. This is known as 'selective reasoning' where you take one thing and bend it to fit your way of life or what you feel is right.

I put this to you, if this was written in scripture over 4500 plus years ago, then it must have been a common occurrence because the authors of the Bible would not address an issue if it was not an issue. So if it was an issue that clearly warranted attention from Bible writers, which I also remind you, that the population of this planet was nowhere near what it is now, then what makes you think that those who practice Zoophilia or secretly participate in these types of activities are really few and far between. Give it time and you will see those numbers increase just like other unnatural behaviors did and will over time. All it takes is for another group to come out of the closest and start fighting for their rights and then another group is sure to follow.

As we progress though this fight, we may see these numbers at somewhere around 22 to 28 percent of Americans by the year 2070ish practicing in some form of zoophilia. It will, just like other unnatural behaviors, be commonplace. Since the other twisted individuals have come out of the closet, then so will these twisted individuals. As the fight continues, and as they are on Capitol Hill with their picket signs and photos of people kissing animals and some even out there with the animals embraced in unity with them, what do you think would happen? Yes, you guessed it, Congress will have no choice but to pass some type of legislation giving these individuals 'their right' to marry or have some type of sexual relationship with animals.

Can you picture it? Can you imagine it? Can you even think about it? Well, aren't you the same person who thought 30 plus years ago that gays and lesbians would never be able to marry? Aren't you the same individual who thought 60 plus years ago that people of different races would never marry? I'm sure you are. Like now you may still think that 50 plus years from now people will not marry animals. Rest assure when I tell you it will happen if we keep going at this rate.

Strange huh? Twisted huh? Sick huh? Unbelievable huh? I think by now you know it's really not.

So where are we going?

Who is coming out of the closest next? Who will pick up the torch? Well we will go to the most twisted and bizarre, back to where we started, to the beginning of this book, but yet the end, Necrophilia.

NECROPHILIA

Well people we are finally here, right where we started. Before we get into any detail on this, let me recap:

It started with Interracial Marriage, then it went to Same Sex Marriage, from there on to Polygamy, soon after Child Molesters or Child Adult Marriage, then it got really twisted and we went to Zoophilia and from there we are here at Necrophilia.

Starting around the year 2080ish which is where we finally are, we got here through a series of fights, protest, marches and laws being passed. We had to continue to accommodate every right and freedom because we compromised ourselves to accommodate one or two groups. This is where we created our own problem. We permitted unnatural behaviors to get to us. We felt in our hearts and minds that if we were to help those engaged in unnatural or unacceptable activities and lifestyles to get their rights, then things would be okay, but things are not okay.

We put our foot in our mouths and we all should be ashamed. Perhaps we should have fought harder to stop the madness early on. It probably would not have made much difference anyway. Remember my saying "Numbers control politics, politics control politicians, politicians control laws, and laws control people". This is why we who are sane individuals would have lost. The numbers just aren't there. So what now? We can talk a little about Necrophilia and give a little history on the subject and see where we are now with this and then we will possibly come up with some alternatives.

Necrophilia is sexual attraction or sexual contact with the dead or corpses. Necrophiliacs, those who practice necrophilia are probably the most twisted of them all. And although rare, there are cases of necrophilia involving some form of homicide so that the individual can gain sexual satisfaction. Most of those involved in this type of behavior will not achieve sexual satisfaction any other way. Accounts in history thus far have been far and between but as we have seen over the past few decades, these numbers too have begun to increase. We can also be sure, that there are hundreds if not thousands of people in the United States who are practicing necrophilia in secrecy, just as those of other unnatural behaviors have done before they too, came out of the closest.

One of the main segments of individuals suffering from necrophilia is serial killers. Some of the world's most prolific serial killers suffered from necrophilia and they include Jeffrey Dahmer, Gary Ridgeway, and British serial killer Dennis Nilsen.

Although necrophilia is considered rare due to there being no real data supporting that there is a significant number of people doing it, it still doesn't change the fact that it is out there and can and has the potential to grow rapidly over time.

Researchers Rosman and Resnick reviewed 122 cases of necrophilia and concluded the following regarding necrophiliacs:

- 68% were motivated by a desire for an unresisting and un-rejecting partner;
- 21% were motivated by a want or desire for reunion with a lost partner;
- 15% were motivated by sexual attraction to dead people;
- 15% were motivated by a desire for comfort or to overcome feelings of isolation; and
- 12% were motivated by a desire to remedy low self-esteem by expressing power over a corpse

Another interesting fact is that those who practice necrophilia still want to have a connection to a dead partner. This is something that could give them even more ammo, basically they can use this in reference to the constitution, that they are still considered married and have every right to do as they will to their dead spouses corpses. After all the constitution wasn't specific, it simply states one man and one woman. It didn't say dead or alive.

Their research also shows that those who participate in necrophilia had occupational access to corpses such as morgue attendants, hospital orderly, and cemetery employees. Go figure. Remember in the previous chapter we spoke about research on those who participate in zoophilia primarily working on farms, well this is similar. There could be a connection between those who work in a particular field that assumes some type of unnatural behavior.

We can even dig deeper into this if we look at those who participate in relationships with children. The majority of those who engage in relationships with children, based on examples in the chapter on child/adult relationships, tend to work with children.

Now if we think about it, as law enforcement crack down on those who are in careers that involve corpses, then as the number of necrophilacs grows, then the alternative will probably be more homicide's and the desecration of corpses. So we can see this could very well be the trigger if you will to persuade lawmakers to act passing laws to legalize this if and (or) when this fight comes to the for-front.

Also, even if we go further, like in the chapter on same-sex marriage, we may even draw a correlation between prisons, where those of the same sex tend to be connected sexually, due to being around those of the same sex for an extended period of time. And even zophilia and beastiallity participates tend to be in a line of work involving animals (farmers, zookeepers, etc.). This could very well be the case in some of our young men and women coming out of prison and changing behavior by being attracted to those of the same sex. So those who are involved in careers where they are around the dead (morgue attendents, cemetary employees etc. are more prone to participate in necrophila behavior. So here we are.

From one thing to the next.

From being a somewhat civil society, to an embarrashment.

From being people of great or good character and morals, to being people without any of these.

From being the leader of good standards for the rest of the world, to not having any.

From fighting for things that truly matter and shaping the face of the planet, to fighting for things that should be criminal in nature.

This is where we are going. Give it time. Some of you may not see these things coming but I indeed do. I am sure that if you really take heed to this book and pay attention to what is going on, then you may open your mind.

Obviously, you can see that this fight will show the least resistance in Congress and the White House, and why should it. We allowed ourselves to get to this point. It is very ironic that the worse of the unnatural behaviors is going to pass its' laws with the least resistance.

Extremely strange huh? Extremely twisted huh? Extremely sick huh? Extremely unbelievable huh? Well, yes it is and there is probably not much we can do about it.

When is enough-enough I put to you?

Where do we draw the line?

Should we have stopped at interracial marriage?

Or should we stop at same sex marriage?

Or maybe even polygamy?

That is about the furthest I am willing to go if at any point it was up to me, but it's not. It is up to all of us. Perhaps, some of you think we should not have ever started at all, even with interracial marriage.

Well maybe we can come up with some ideas and shed some light on things in our conclusion.

CONCLUSION

In conclusion, I want to start by a reference made by a famous boxer. Most would say that he is the greatest of all times, Muhammad Ali. Muhammad Ali did an interview once and spoke about some of the things I talked about in this book. During the interview Mr. Ali was only referencing interracial marriages but I am going to use it in a different way.

Let me start by asking a question to each and every one of you.

What is the most intelligent species on the planet? Well, it shouldn't take you long to answer but just in case you didn't know, it is HUMANS.

Now let me put a series of questions to you. This series of questions relate to all other species, not to humans.

Series 1

Have you ever seen two male birds mate? Have you ever seen two female sheep mate? Have you ever seen two male alligators mate? Have you ever seen two female wales mate? Have you ever seen two male lions mate? Have you ever seen two female monkeys mate?

Series 2

Have you ever seen an adult female cat mate with a male kitten? Have you ever seen an adult male Pig mate with a female piglet? Have you ever seen an adult female dog mate with a male puppy? Have you ever seen an adult male bear mate with a baby female bear?

Series 3

Have you ever seen a Hippo mate with a tiger? Have you ever seen a giraffe mate with a rabbit? Have you ever seen an elephant mate with a horse? Have you ever seen a shark mate with a crocodile?

Series 4

Have you ever seen a live snake mate with a dead snake? Have you ever seen a live wildebeest mate with a dead wildebeest? Have you ever seen a live dolphin mate with a dead dolphin?

Series 5

Have you ever seen an adult female polar bear mate with her blood born son? Have you ever seen an adult male zebra mate with his blood born daughter? Have you ever seen a female kangaroo mate with her blood born brother? Have you ever seen a male monkey mate with his female sister?

I am guessing your answer is NO to most, if not all, of these questions. The reason being is because they, meaning animals, consider these actions to be unnatural in nature. If we look at this realistically, how can we as humans (the so called most intelligent species on the planet) not consider these lifestyles and activities to be unnatural as well. If we send men to the moon, walk upright, build skyscrapers, build airplanes, discover gravity, break the sound barrier, send rovers to mars, discover cures for diseases, do open heart surgeries, and write books, then why is it so difficult for us to not participate in behaviors that are deemed unacceptable even to animals. Animals, who we have as pets and are subjective and somewhat slaves to us share a stronger moral compass than do humans. If it is all unnatural behavior to them, then it should very well be unnatural behavior to us. After all, we rule the planet and set the trends.

So now let us look at the Biblical perspective of these things. I am not going to preach to you. We will only take a look at the book of Leviticus 18:22-23, in verse 22 reads "Thou shall not lie with mankind, as with womankind: it is an abomination." The word abomination is a word that the bible uses frequently to describe activity beyond sin. We all know what sin is but if something is an abomination to the Almighty, then that means it really sickens him. In other words it is worse than sin itself. Fred Price Jr. describes abominations as activities that came to the planet after the fall of (Lucifer) Satan and the rest of the angels who were kicked out of heaven. He goes on further to say that an abomination leaves a foul order or stench in the nostrils of the Almighty. So why would anyone want to make the Almighty really look down on them by participating in certain types of behaviors. Let me re-iterate, I am not attacking anyone. I am simply making points here. You are all human beings and you have your own beliefs and that is your own free will. I will always respect that.

Verse 23 reads "Neither shall thou lie with any beast to defile thyself therewith: neither shall any women stand before a beast to lie down thereto: it is confusion. This is yet just another verse speaking of unnatural behavior. It is a direct reference to zoophilia. Again, even the Almighty is against unnatural behaviors.

One interesting thing about this is that even back in Biblical times all these unnatural behaviors existed. This should confirm that these behaviors are not new. Even more shocking is that unnatural behaviors perhaps may have been the reason for the great flood of Noah, to cleanse the earth. Think about it, as bad as things are going now around the world, it's still not bad enough for God or the source to wipe away or cleanse the planet. This should tell us that it was much worse then. In other words, all these unnatural behaviors would have been quite common at that time.

We can even quote Fred Price Jr again by saying "that the abnormal was the normal". So when abnormal behavior becomes normal, then we condition our minds to accept it and that abnormal behavior now becomes acceptable. A perfect example of this would be black on black crime in most of the larger urban communities across America. Some 40 plus years ago this would have been unacceptable behavior as well. There is no way anyone could have predicted that it would get this bad, but it has and we have somehow conditioned ourselves to accepting it. We are not really doing much as a country to stop it.

Some of these unnatural behaviors may and should possibly be accepted but the problem is if we accept one, at some point, we may have to accept another and another, because more and more people will come out in support of it as time progresses. Remember my saying "Numbers control politics, politics control politicians, politicians control laws, and laws control people". So if the numbers are there, then we cannot win the fight. The only way to fight some of these unnatural behaviors is to educate others, as well as ourselves in order to attempt to keep our children from making unwise sexual decisions that will cause more harm than good. We should work to keep some of these behaviors out of the mainstream media. Kids are so impressionable and they pick up on things and run with what's 'in' most of the time.

So where are we going? Who's up next? Who's waiting? Well, perhaps spirits, ghost, entities, aliens, and demons? Think it won't or hasn't happened? Stay tuned for another book.

REFERENCES

Hucker, S. J. (2012). Forensic Psychiatry. ca. Retrieved from http://www.forensicpsychiatry.ca/paraphilia/necro.htm

Source: (12/16/2014). Interracial Marriage Laws, Head, Tom. (online), 12/05/2014 http://civilliberty.about.com/od/raceequalopportunity/tp/Interracial-Marriage-Laws-History-Timeline.htm

Source: Guess Who's Coming to Dinner. Dir. William Rose. 1967 Film.

Source: Star Trek, The series. Dir. Gene Roddenberry. 1968.

http://www.pewresearch.org/fact-tank/2015/06/12/interracial-marriage-who-is-marrying-out/

Source: (n.o.). Bower, Lisa. Life123 The History of Same Sex Marriages. (online). 2/5/2015 http://quod.lib.umich.edu/cgi/t/text/text-idx?cc=mfsfront;c=mfs;c=mfsfront;idno=ark5583.0020.001;rgn=main;view=text;xc=1;g=mfsg

https://www.congress.gov/bill/104th-congress/house-bill/3396/text

Congress.Gov Library of Congress Section H.R.3396 - Defense of Marriage Act 1996

Source: The Pursuit of Holiness, Fred Price Jr

Source: (Leviticus 18:23, King James Version)

http://www.nytimes.com/2015/06/27/us/
supreme-court-same-sex-marriage.html?_r=0

InfidelityFacts.com http://www.infidelityfacts.
com/index.html 2006

Source: (4/10/20014). The Pursuit of Holiness,
Price Jr, Fred. 3/4/2015 FJ208a & b FJ109a & b

Source: (2/27/2012). Divorce and the LDS
Church. (online), 12/30/2015 http://www.
religioustolerance.org/lds_divo.htm

Source: (1998-2015). Creating Safer Havens.
(online), 1/12/2015http://creatingsaferhavens.
com/news.html

Source: (1/23/2013). Leah Shipman, Ex-Teacher,
Marries North Carolina Student She Was Accused

Of Having Sex With, The Huffington Post. (online). 1/15/2015 http://www.huffingtonpost.com/2013/01/21/leah-shipman-ex-teacher-marries-student_n_2521118.html

Source: (10/15/2009). Doctor's incestuous relationship produced son. (online), 11/23/2014 http://www.smh.com.au/national/doctors-incestuous-relationship-produced-son-20091014-gxfl.html

Source: (06/22/2012).Mother charged with incest with 16 year old son gets under 4 years claims "genetic attraction".(online).1/4/2014 http://www.inquisitr.com/261002/mother-charged-with-incest-with-16-year-old-son-gets-under-4-years-claims-genetic-attraction/

Source: (3/5/2014). Sister accused of incest with brother rearrested on charge of choking husband. (online), 3/8/2014 http://www.chron.com/news/houston-texas/texas/article/Sister-accused-of-incest-with-brother-rearrested-5290546.php

Source: (1989). Sexual Attraction to Corpses: A Psychiatric Review of Necrophilia. (online), 10/12/2014 www.jaapl.org/content/17/2/153.full.pdf

CPSIA information can be obtained
at www.ICGtesting.com
Printed in the USA
LVOW12s1030050416
482231LV00001BA/11/P